SCHOLASTIC

Success With Addition & Subtraction

New York • Toronto • London • Auckland • Sydney
Mexico City • New Delhi • Hong Kong • Buenos Aires

Teaching Resources

State Standards Correlations

To find out how this book helps you meet your state's standards,
log on to **www.scholastic.com/ssw**

Written by Danette Randolph
Cover design by Ka-Yeon Kim-Li
Interior illustrations by Kathy Marlin
Interior design by Quack & Company

ISBN-13 978-0-545-20096-7
ISBN-10 0-545-20096-2

1 2 3 4 5 6 7 8 9 10   40   17 16 15 14 13 12 11 10

Introduction

Parents and teachers alike will find this book to be a valuable learning tool. Students will enjoy completing a wide variety of math activities that are both engaging and educational. Take a look at the Table of Contents and you will feel rewarded providing such a valuable resource for your students.

Table of Contents

Columbus Sailed the Ocean Blue

 In 1492, Columbus sailed to America with these ships: the *Pinta*, the *Nina*, and the *Santa Maria*. Add the number of these ships to the number of ships in the picture.

 Scholastic Success With Addition & Subtraction • Grade 3

Name _____

Packing for Plymouth

Subtract. Then use the code to write a letter for each difference to see what the Pilgrims packed for Plymouth. Put an X on the item the Pilgrims did not pack.

15 − 1	16 − 8	15 − 13	13 − 8	16 − 5		7 − 5	15 − 8	17 − 6
○	○	○	○	○		○	○	○

18 − 14	11 − 9	17 − 12	16 − 15	17 − 0
○	○	○	○	○

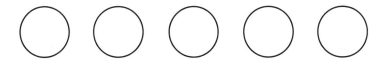

18 − 4	10 − 8	18 − 8	12 − 1	15 − 11
○	○	○	○	○

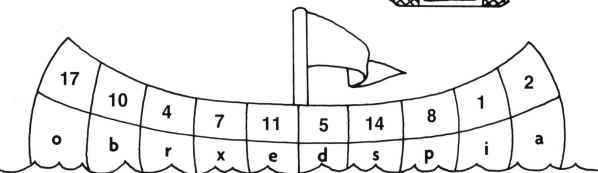

17	10	4	7	11	5	14	8	1	2
o	b	r	x	e	d	s	p	i	a

On the *Mayflower*

Add or subtract. Write the Pilgrims' names in alphabetical order by sequencing the answers from greatest to smallest.

Resolve	14 − 7 =
Susan	13 − 9 =
Jasper	6 + 7 =
Priscilla	8 + 2 =
Edward	9 + 6 =
Solomon	11 − 6 =
Prudence	18 − 9 =
Constance	8 + 8 =
Remember	17 − 9 =
Oceanus	7 + 5 =
Thomas	15 − 12 =
Samuel	14 − 8 =
Charity	6 + 12 =
Peregrine	16 − 5 =
Humility	9 + 5 =

_____

_____

_____

_____

_____

_____

_____

_____

_____

_____

Which name would your name follow in the alphabetical list of names? Write a number sentence to show where your name would follow.

Great States

Add or subtract. Connect the matching answers to find each state's shape.

Delaware	16 − 9 =
Massachusetts	7 + 7 =
New Hampshire	15 − 6 =
New York	17 + 1 =
South Carolina	14 − 3 =
Maryland	15 − 2 =
Pennsylvania	14 − 9 =
Connecticut	12 + 5 =
Rhode Island	7 + 3 =
North Carolina	13 − 7 =
Georgia	7 + 5 =
New Jersey	14 − 6 =
Virginia	7 + 8 =

4 + 3 =

7 + 2 =

$$\begin{array}{r} 9 \\ + 9 \\ \hline \end{array}$$

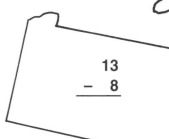
$$\begin{array}{r} 13 \\ - 8 \\ \hline \end{array}$$

$$\begin{array}{r} 6 \\ + 5 \\ \hline \end{array}$$

8 + 5 =

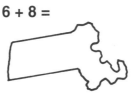
6 + 8 =

$$\begin{array}{r} 18 \\ - 6 \\ \hline \end{array}$$

17 − 7 =

18 − 1 =

12 − 4 =

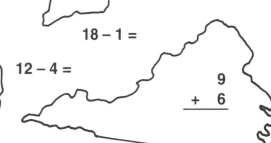
$$\begin{array}{r} 15 \\ - 9 \\ \hline \end{array}$$
$$\begin{array}{r} 9 \\ + 6 \\ \hline \end{array}$$

Let Freedom Ring

Add. Use the code to write words that tell about our past.

63 + 12	12 + 11	65 + 33	62 + 24	34 + 13	24 + 10	41 + 34	53 + 46

◯ ◯ ◯ ◯ ◯ ◯ ◯ ◯

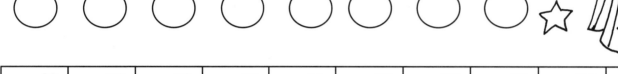

40 + 46	26 + 72	23 + 10	35 + 43	21 + 43	53 + 34	22 + 10	13 + 34	64 + 14	68 + 31

◯ ◯ ◯ ◯ ◯ ◯ ◯ ◯ ◯ ◯

31 + 33	25 + 22	21 + 30	44 + 54	76 + 10	21 + 11	11 + 10

◯ ◯ ◯ ◯ ◯ ◯ ◯

40 + 11	35 + 63	44 + 20	52 + 12

◯ ◯ ◯ ◯

Code

21 Y	23 M	32 T	33 V	34 C	42 P	47 I	51 B
64 L	69 D	75 A	78 O	86 R	87 U	98 E	99 N

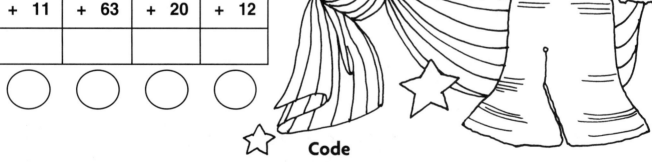

Name _____

Moving West

Subtract. Follow the even sums to guide the settlers to their new home.

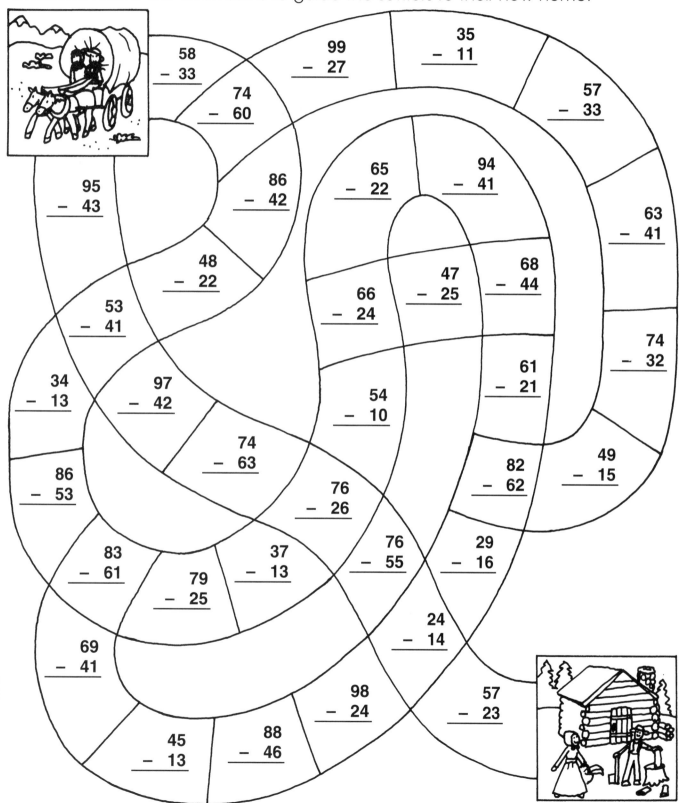

United We Stand

Add or subtract. Color answers greater than 50 green to show the United States.
Color answers less than 50 blue.

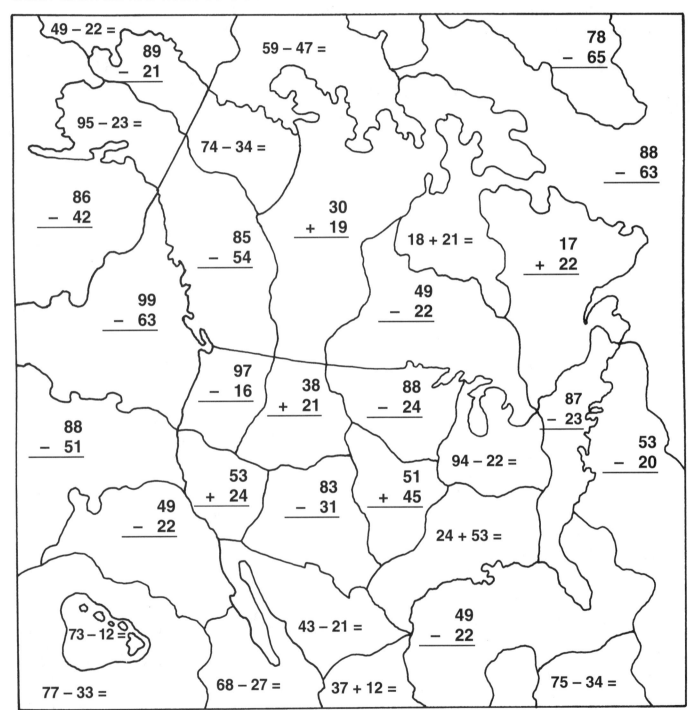

49 − 22 =

89
− 21

59 − 47 =

78
− 65

95 − 23 =

74 − 34 =

88
− 63

86
− 42

30
+ 19

18 + 21 =

17
+ 22

85
− 54

99
− 63

49
− 22

97
− 16

38
+ 21

88
− 24

87
− 23

88
− 51

53
− 20

53
+ 24

83
− 31

51
+ 45

94 − 22 =

49
− 22

24 + 53 =

73 − 12 =

49
− 22

77 − 33 =

43 − 21 =

68 − 27 =

37 + 12 =

75 − 34 =

 **Can you find Hawaii in the map above? Write an addition problem that has the
same answer.**

Stars and Stripes Forever

Circle groups of 10. Write the number of tens and ones. Write the number in the star.

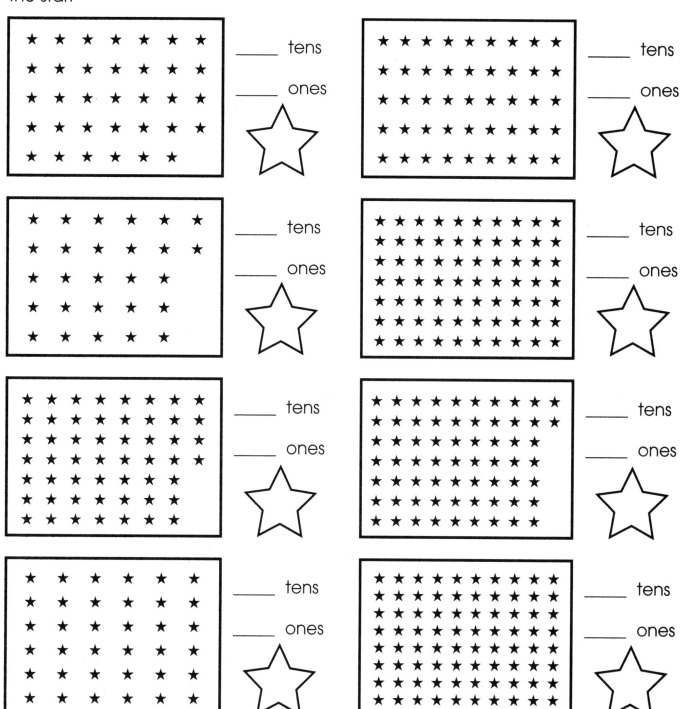

_____ tens

_____ ones

_____ tens

_____ ones

_____ tens

_____ ones

_____ tens

_____ ones

_____ tens

_____ ones

_____ tens

_____ ones

_____ tens

_____ ones

_____ tens

_____ ones

 Find out how many stars were on the first flag. On another piece of paper, add that number to the number of stars on the United States flag today. How many groups of tens and ones are there?

Name _____

The U.S. Capital

Add. Match each building to the correct sum.

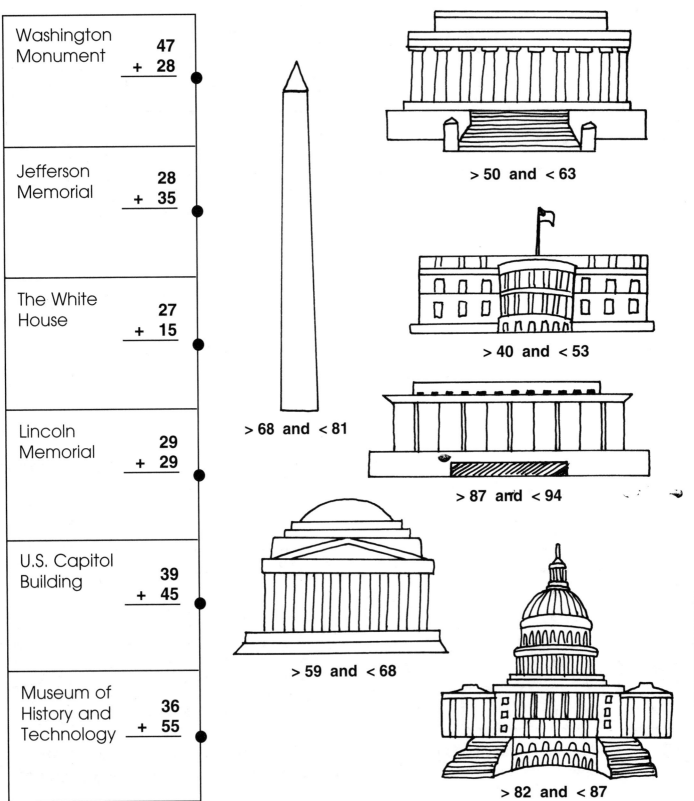

Washington Monument	47 + 28
Jefferson Memorial	28 + 35
The White House	27 + 15
Lincoln Memorial	29 + 29
U.S. Capitol Building	39 + 45
Museum of History and Technology	36 + 55

> 50 and < 63

> 40 and < 53

> 87 and < 94

> 68 and < 81

> 59 and < 68

> 82 and < 87

Name _____

Mr. President

Add. Write the letters in the circles to identify each president.

I was a leader in the Civil War.

39 + 13	38 + 15	56 + 26	26 + 35	29 + 67	27 + 25	43 + 39

◯ ◯ ◯ ◯ ◯ ◯ ◯

I helped write the Declaration of Independence.

19 + 18	28 + 55	24 + 18	19 + 23	17 + 66	59 + 19	49 + 15	78 + 18	48 + 34

◯ ◯ ◯ ◯ ◯ ◯ ◯ ◯ ◯

I was a leader in the American Revolutionary War.

59 + 39	48 + 24	27 + 37	19 + 46	27 + 26	38 + 44	27 + 18	18 + 29	38 + 58	27 + 55

◯ ◯ ◯ ◯ ◯ ◯ ◯ ◯ ◯ ◯

Code

61 C	98 W	55 Y	83 E	45 G	82 N	78 R	65 H	52 L
96 O	42 F	86 K	47 T	72 A	37 J	64 S	53 I	36 D

 On another piece of paper, make a code and write problems for the name of our current president.

Travel the Nation

Look at the number on each form of transportation. Write the number of tens and ones. Regroup. Write the new number.

Great Vacations

Subtract. Draw a line from each difference to the vacation spot on the map.

Mount Rushmore	Niagara Falls	Gateway Arch	Four Corners Monument	Statue of Liberty
72 − 27	57 − 29	58 − 39	93 − 19	94 − 29

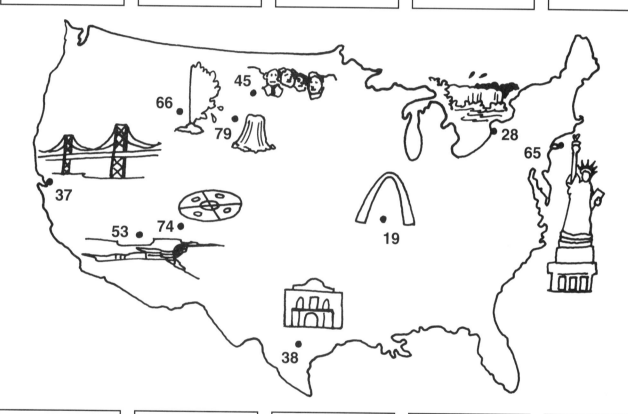

Grand Canyon	Devil's Tower	Golden Gate Bridge	The Alamo	Old Faithful
82 − 29	93 − 14	64 − 27	66 − 28	94 − 28

 On the map above, mark and write the name of a vacation spot in the United States you would like to visit. Write a subtraction problem for it.

Name _____

The Nation's Weather

City	High	Low
Anchorage	52°	13°
Chicago	68°	29°
Indianapolis	76°	48°
Newark	68°	39°
Orlando	90°	61°
St. Louis	81°	42°
San Francisco	75°	49°
Seattle	72°	37°

Find the difference between the high and low temperature in each city.

Anchorage	Chicago	Indianapolis	Newark	Orlando	St. Louis	San Francisco	Seattle
52 – 13 39							

Find the difference between:

San Francisco high and Chicago low	Orlando high and Anchorage low
Anchorage high and Indianapolis low	St. Louis high and Newark low
Seattle high and San Francisco low	Indianapolis high and Seattle low

Cooling Off

Read each thermometer. Subtract to find the new temperature.

23°	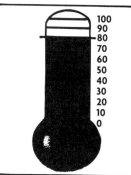	58°	
51°		35°	
12°		64°	
47°		26°	

Name _____

America's Favorite Pastime

Add or subtract. Use the chart to color the picture.

white	blue	brown	red	yellow
0–20	21–40	41–60	61–80	81–100

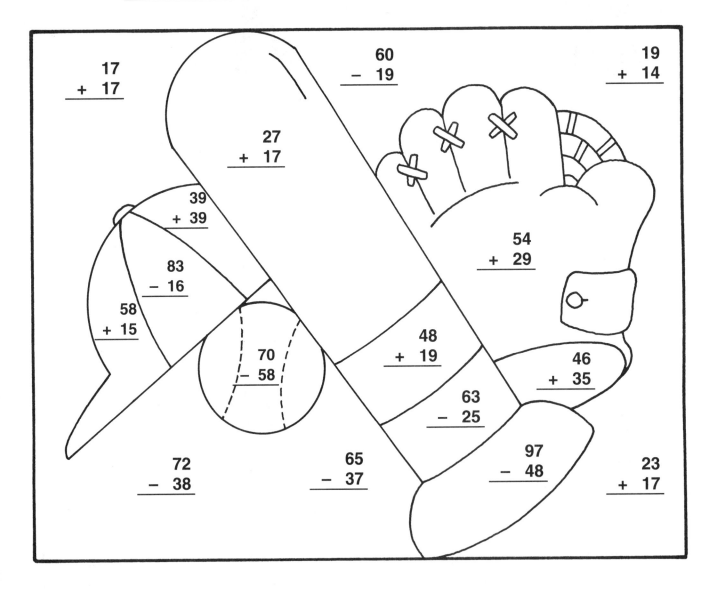

 Finish the pattern.

32   34   36   42   46

Name _____

High-Scoring Game

	1	2	3	4	5	6	7	8	9
Cardinals	16	57	91	39	68	25	83	44	72
Blue Jays	87	11	45	94	29	73	32	58	66

Find the total number of runs in each inning.

Add.

1	2	3	4	5	6	7	8	9
16 +87								

Find the difference in runs in each inning.

Subtract.

1	2	3	4	5	6	7	8	9
87 −16								

Solve.

A. How many runs did the Cardinals score altogether in the first and sixth inning?

_____ runs

B. How many runs did the Blue Jays score altogether in the seventh and eighth inning?

_____ runs

C. How many more runs did the Cardinals score in the third inning than the second inning?

_____ runs

D. How many more runs did the Blue Jays score in the first inning than the fifth inning?

_____ runs

Name _____

More Fun Sports

Add or subtract.

91 − 67	48 + 43	92 − 45	70 − 17	63 − 47	38 + 54	29 + 36	80 − 42
skating	football	hockey	volleyball	basketball	soccer	tennis	track

Complete the puzzle with the sport that goes with each answer.

Down
1. 47
2. 53
3. 24
5. 38

Across
3. 92
4. 16
5. 65
6. 91

Choose your favorite sport from above. On another piece of paper, write a problem with its same answer. Try to write a problem that includes regrouping.

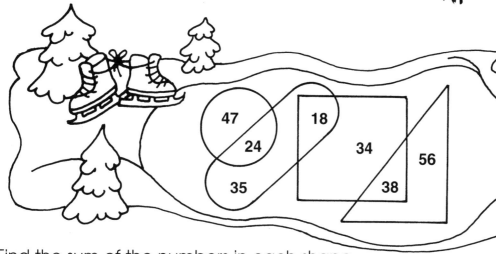

Find the sum of the numbers in each shape.

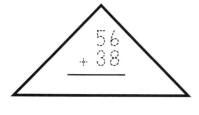

$$\begin{array}{r} 56 \\ + 38 \\ \hline \end{array}$$

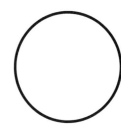

Use the sums from above to solve.

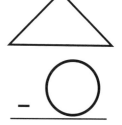

Find the difference between the greatest
number in the ◯ and the greatest
number in the ▢ .

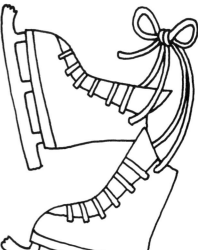

Find the difference between the greatest
number in the △ and the smallest
number in the ◯ .

**On another piece of paper, find
the sum of all the numbers in the
shapes on the skating pond.**

Great Math Inventions

Add or subtract. Then write the problem's letter above its matching answer below.

S.   29
     + 46

I.   48
     – 24

A.   27
     + 38

R.   56
     – 18

R.   37
     + 47

W.   81
     – 24

H.   23
     + 35

I.   90
     – 26

U.   52
     – 19

O.   37
     + 35

L.   70
     – 19

M.   82
     – 48

B.   23
     + 48

L.   52
     + 28

G.   91
     – 22

U.   73
     – 25

___ ___ ___ ___ ___ ___ ___   ___ ___ ___ ___ ___ ___ ___ ___ ___
57 24 80 51 64 65 34   71 48 84 38 72 33 69 58 75

invented and patented the adding machine in St. Louis, Missouri, in 1888.

Name _____

It All Adds Up!

Add. Fill in the missing numbers.

3 2 4 + 6 3 □ —— □ □ 6	2 4 □ + □ 5 1 —— 7 □ 2	□ 5 5 + 3 □ 1 —— 4 8 □	2 □ 3 + □ 1 3 —— 5 2 □
4 1 □ + 3 □ 2 —— □ 3 7	□ 4 3 + 1 4 □ —— 2 □ 9	2 □ □ + 2 1 6 —— □ 1 8	□ 3 1 + 4 □ □ —— 8 5 3
1 □ 2 + □ 3 3 —— 3 7 □	□ 4 1 + 1 3 □ —— 6 □ 5	3 3 □ + □ □ 3 —— 6 6 8	□ 1 2 + 2 □ 2 —— 9 4 □
2 2 □ + 3 1 4 —— □ □ 4	5 □ 4 + □ 3 4 —— 8 4 □	2 2 4 + 1 □ 3 —— □ 6 □	□ 1 6 + 1 3 □ —— 5 □ 8

Joe and Ellie were going to the movies. Joe brought \$5.□0, and Ellie brought \$□.35. If they had \$9.75 altogether, how much money did they each have? Show your work.

Name _____

It's Electrifying!

Regroup tens into hundreds. Draw a line to connect.

TENS

53

o

29

TENS

76

o

41

TENS

85

o

26

TENS

44

o

38

5 hundreds
3 tens

7 hundreds
6 tens

2 hundreds
9 tens

3 hundreds
8 tens

4 hundreds
4 tens

4 hundreds
1 ten

8 hundreds
5 tens

2 hundreds
6 tens

Fill in each missing number.

hundreds	tens	ones	number
200	40	7	2 4 7
400	70	6	__ __ __
300		2	__ 9 __
100	90		__ __ 3
500		1	__ 6 __

Let the Light Shine

Regroup hundreds to tens.

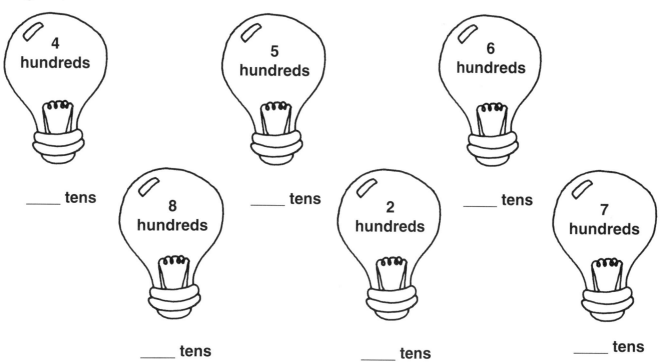

Color the lightbulb in each box with the greater value yellow.

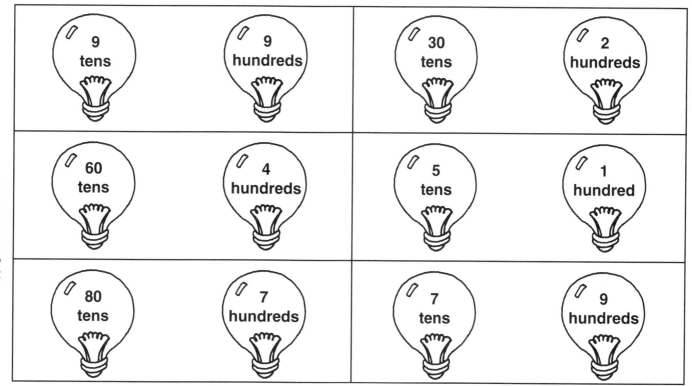

Name _____

A, B, C, . . .

Add.

286 + 668	138 + 289	285 + 269
496 + 188	159 + 190	175 + 189
499 + 446	375 + 469	183 + 289
299 + 158	196 + 378	657 + 285
186 + 287	157 + 267	276 + 566

295 + 675	188 + 185	487 + 385
284 + 439	389 + 188	595 + 289
128 + 379	297 + 179	198 + 199
365 + 378	192 + 579	123 + 589
386 + 189	295 + 379	436 + 538

This letter sounds like a question.

Color each answer with a 4 in the ones place to see!

This letter names a feature on your face.

Color each answer with a 7 in the tens place to see!

Name _____

. . . X, Y, and X

Add.

PXNOVTRQZ
WNOUTRYS

298 + 276	191 + 343	269 + 289
157 + 189	137 + 369	278 + 485
395 + 457	244 + 279	499 + 446
288 + 664	236 + 288	577 + 388
498 + 399	399 + 164	284 + 439

259 + 467	364 + 258	487 + 436
199 + 128	199 + 89	238 + 287
255 + 373	509 + 315	117 + 304
257 + 569	276 + 566	149 + 279
339 + 385	258 + 467	179 + 348

This letter names an icy drink.

Color each answer with a 5 in the
hundreds place to see!

This letter names an insect that stings.

Color each answer with a 2 in the
tens place to see!

Name _____

Let's Talk

Find the number that goes with
each letter on the phone. Subtract.

Phone keypad:
1   ABC 2   DEF 3
GHI 4   JKL 5   MNO 6
PQRS 7   TUV 8   WXYZ 9

JDH
– A P L   –

G M Q
– C S V   –

E W A
– B Y N   –

M A L
– F N O   –

W T U
– J V W   –

R E K
– D M P   –

T J I
– E X Q   –

K N H
– H Z U   –

F D X
– B G Y   –

 Find the numbers for your name. Add to find the sum of the numbers.

Name _____

Out of This World

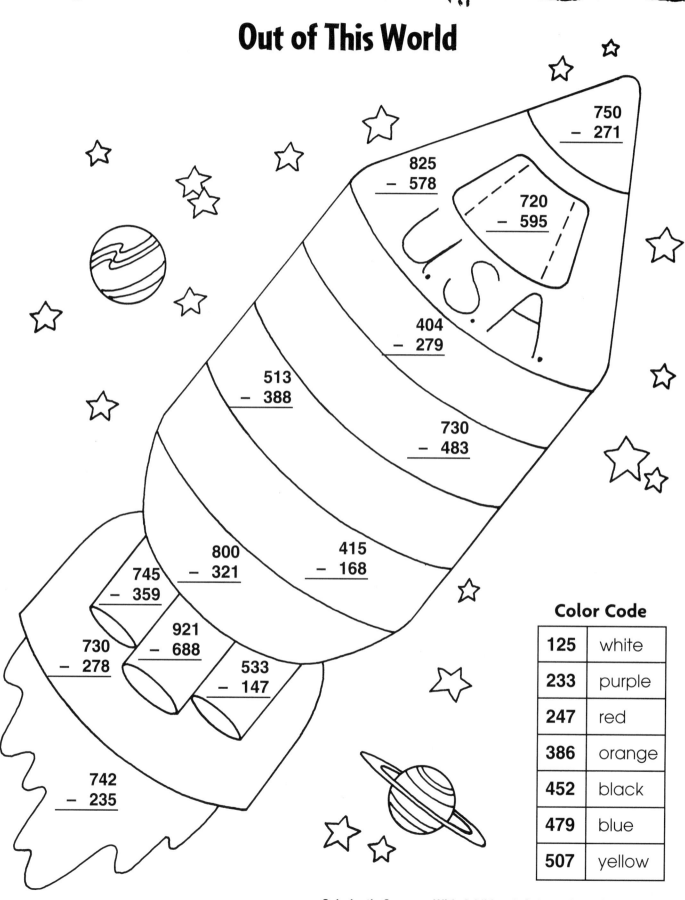

750
− 271

825
− 578

720
− 595

404
− 279

513
− 388

730
− 483

800
− 321

415
− 168

745
− 359

921
− 688

730
− 278

533
− 147

742
− 235

Color Code

125	white
233	purple
247	red
386	orange
452	black
479	blue
507	yellow

Name _____

Adding/subtracting 3-digit numbers with regrouping

Ride Through the Clouds

Add or subtract.

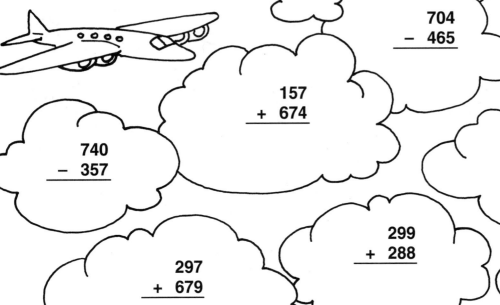

```
      704        832
    - 465      - 317

      157        146
    + 674      + 578

  740          299        259
- 357        + 288      + 489

    297
  + 679

  904          823
- 435        - 649
                          297
                        + 397
```

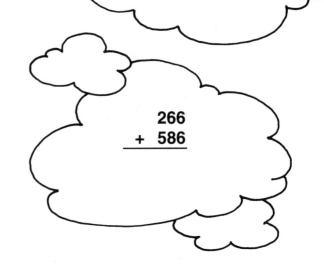

```
  266
+ 586
```

Use the color code to color each cloud.
Begin with the smallest answer (1st) and
end with the largest answer (12th).

1st	red	7th	pink
2nd	orange	8th	white
3rd	yellow	9th	black
4th	green	10th	brown
5th	blue	11th	gray
6th	purple	12th	peach

Copyright © Scholastic Inc.

Mailbox Mix-Up

Add or subtract. Match each person to the correct mailbox sum.

My mailbox has a 4, 9, and 3. The 9 is in the ones place.

My mailbox has a 7, 6, and 2. The 2 is in the hundreds place.

My mailbox has a 1, 5, and 5. The 1 is in the ones place.

My mailbox has a 4, 9, and 3. The 9 is in the hundreds place.

My mailbox has a 2, 7, and 6. The 2 is in the ones place.

My mailbox has a 5, 1, and 5. The 1 is in the hundreds place.

My mailbox has a 4, 9, and 3. The 9 is in the tens place.

My mailbox has a 5, 5, and 1. The 1 is in the tens place.

My mailbox has a 2, 7, and 6. The 2 is in the tens place.

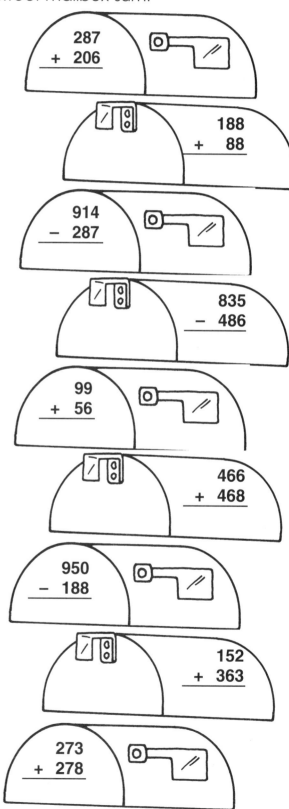

$$287 + 206$$

$$188 + 88$$

$$914 - 287$$

$$835 - 486$$

$$99 + 56$$

$$466 + 468$$

$$950 - 188$$

$$152 + 363$$

$$273 + 278$$

Name _____

Your Part of the World

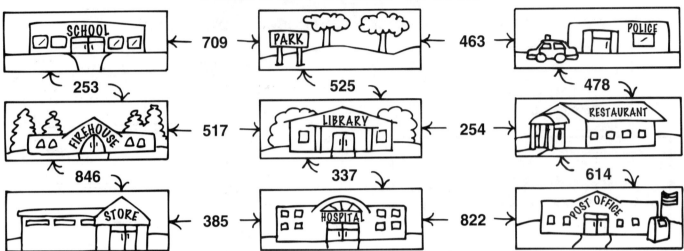

Use the distance between each building to solve each problem.

A. How many feet is it from the firehouse to the library to the park?	**B.** How many feet is it from the post office to the restaurant to the police station?	**C.** How many feet is it from the park to the school to the firehouse?

D. Which way is the shortest route— from the store to the firehouse to the library or from the store to the hospital to the library? Circle.

$$\begin{array}{r} 846 \\ +\ 517 \\ \hline \end{array} \qquad \begin{array}{r} 385 \\ +\ 337 \\ \hline \end{array}$$

E. How much farther is the

school to the park than the store to the hospital?	firehouse to the library than the park to the police station?	library to the park than the hospital to the store?

 On another piece of paper, find which route is the shortest way from the school to the post office. Trace this route on the map above.

Copyright © Scholastic Inc.

Home Sweet Home

Use the coordinates to find each number. Add or subtract.

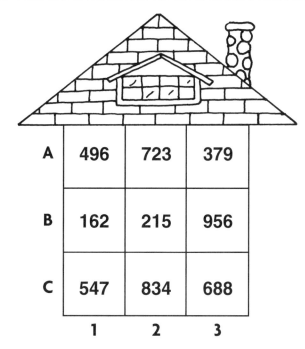

A	496	723	379
B	162	215	956
C	547	834	688
	1	2	3

E	668	884	345
F	239	716	188
G	422	578	957
	4	5	6

A. (A, 1)
(F, 6) − ___

B. (B, 3)
(E, 4) − ___

C. (C, 1)
(F, 4) + ___

D. (A, 3)
(E, 6) + ___

E. (A, 2)
(B, 1) − ___

F. (G, 4)
(B, 2) − ___

G. (G, 6)
(C, 3) − ___

H. (E, 5)
(C, 2) + ___

I. (B, 3)
(G, 5) − ___

 Color the largest number on each house orange. Color the smallest number on each house purple.

Name _____

What a Beautiful World!

Add or subtract.

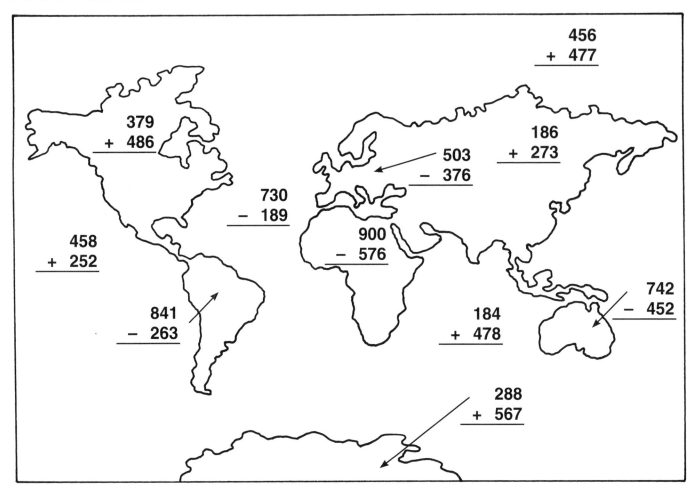

Label the map using the code below.

North America	> 860 and < 927	Atlantic Ocean	> 496 and < 560
South America	> 571 and < 658	Indian Ocean	> 581 and < 672
Australia	> 189 and < 293	Pacific Ocean	> 671 and < 732
Asia	> 423 and < 538	Arctic Ocean	> 867 and < 948
Europe	> 85 and < 266		
Antarctica	> 748 and < 864		
Africa	> 297 and < 334		

Add the answers for the oceans together.

Majestic Mountains

Add or subtract. Use the code to name four
different mountain ranges.

N	6,348
R	8,789
A	5,063
I	7,695
O	2,429
K	5,642
E	7,483
C	3,012
Y	2,351
Z	5,234
L	3,721
U	6,704
P	3,827
S	8,749
D	4,907

```
  2,033        2,411        2,504        4,328
+ 3,030      + 1,310      + 1,323      + 4,421
```

◯   ◯   ◯   ◯

```
  4,258        1,326        1,012        2,321        1,231
+ 4,531      + 1,103      + 2,000      + 3,321      + 1,120
```

◯   ◯   ◯   ◯   ◯

```
  1,204        2,113        2,042        3,746        4,131
+ 1,225      + 3,121      + 3,021      + 5,043      + 1,511
```

◯   ◯   ◯   ◯   ◯

```
  4,053        2,216        2,506        6,471        7,326
+ 1,010      + 4,132      + 2,401      + 1,012      + 1,423
```

◯   ◯   ◯   ◯   ◯

Reach for the Top

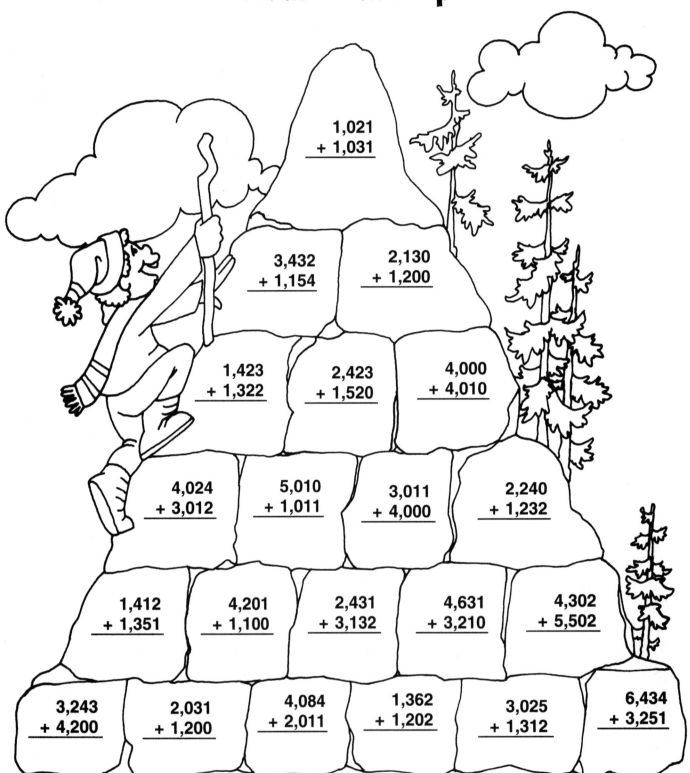

$$
\begin{array}{r} 1,021 \\ +\ 1,031 \\ \hline \end{array}
$$

$$
\begin{array}{r} 3,432 \\ +\ 1,154 \\ \hline \end{array}
\qquad
\begin{array}{r} 2,130 \\ +\ 1,200 \\ \hline \end{array}
$$

$$
\begin{array}{r} 1,423 \\ +\ 1,322 \\ \hline \end{array}
\qquad
\begin{array}{r} 2,423 \\ +\ 1,520 \\ \hline \end{array}
\qquad
\begin{array}{r} 4,000 \\ +\ 4,010 \\ \hline \end{array}
$$

$$
\begin{array}{r} 4,024 \\ +\ 3,012 \\ \hline \end{array}
\qquad
\begin{array}{r} 5,010 \\ +\ 1,011 \\ \hline \end{array}
\qquad
\begin{array}{r} 3,011 \\ +\ 4,000 \\ \hline \end{array}
\qquad
\begin{array}{r} 2,240 \\ +\ 1,232 \\ \hline \end{array}
$$

$$
\begin{array}{r} 1,412 \\ +\ 1,351 \\ \hline \end{array}
\qquad
\begin{array}{r} 4,201 \\ +\ 1,100 \\ \hline \end{array}
\qquad
\begin{array}{r} 2,431 \\ +\ 3,132 \\ \hline \end{array}
\qquad
\begin{array}{r} 4,631 \\ +\ 3,210 \\ \hline \end{array}
\qquad
\begin{array}{r} 4,302 \\ +\ 5,502 \\ \hline \end{array}
$$

$$
\begin{array}{r} 3,243 \\ +\ 4,200 \\ \hline \end{array}
\qquad
\begin{array}{r} 2,031 \\ +\ 1,200 \\ \hline \end{array}
\qquad
\begin{array}{r} 4,084 \\ +\ 2,011 \\ \hline \end{array}
\qquad
\begin{array}{r} 1,362 \\ +\ 1,202 \\ \hline \end{array}
\qquad
\begin{array}{r} 3,025 \\ +\ 1,312 \\ \hline \end{array}
\qquad
\begin{array}{r} 6,434 \\ +\ 3,251 \\ \hline \end{array}
$$

Write an addition problem with four numbers in the answer so the sum of the digits equals 12.

One in a Thousand

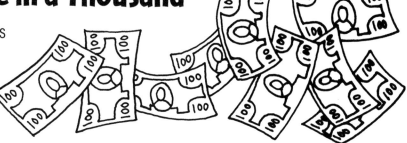

Add. Write the letters on the lines below in order from the smallest to the largest sums to find out whose face is on the hundred-dollar bill.

F. $27.41
+ $12.55

N. $59.63
+ $20.33

N. $85.42
+ $14.06

R. $31.75
+ $35.24

K. $64.84
+ $22.15

A. $29.35
+ $50.42

L. $46.96
+ $42.03

I. $73.57
+ $23.43

_ _ _ _ _ _ _ _ _ _ _

If you have **50** hundred-dollar bills, you have _____ thousand dollars!

If you have **20** hundred-dollar bills, you have _____ thousand dollars!

If you have **80** hundred-dollar bills, you have _____ thousand dollars!

If you have **10** hundred-dollar bills, you have _____ thousand dollars!

If you have **30** hundred-dollar bills, you have _____ thousand dollars!

If you have **70** hundred-dollar bills, you have _____ thousand dollars!

If you have **90** hundred-dollar bills, you have _____ thousand dollars!

If you have **40** hundred-dollar bills, you have _____ thousand dollars!

If you have **60** hundred-dollar bills, you have _____ thousand dollars!

Great Beginnings

Add. Look at each sum. Use the code below to color the picture.

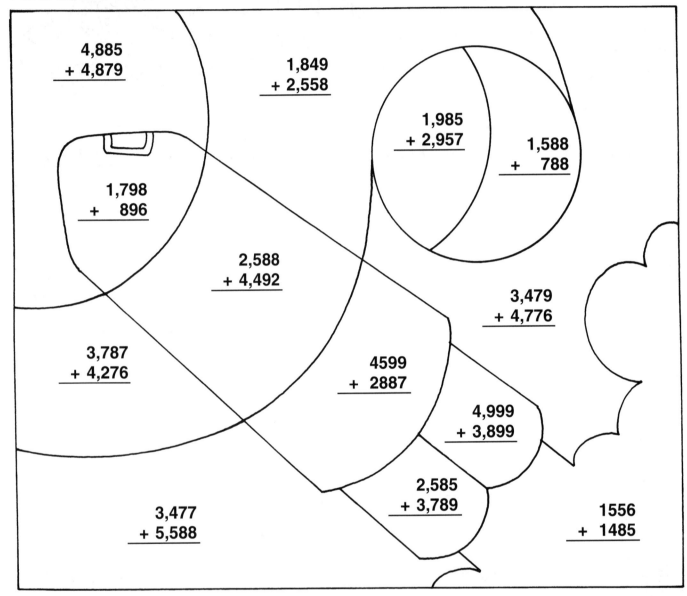

4,885
+ 4,879

1,849
+ 2,558

1,985
+ 2,957

1,588
+   788

1,798
+   896

2,588
+ 4,492

3,479
+ 4,776

3,787
+ 4,276

4599
+ 2887

4,999
+ 3,899

3,477
+ 5,588

2,585
+ 3,789

1556
+ 1485

4,942 — blue
2,694 — white
8,898 — black
7,080 — white

8,063 — blue
7,486 — white
6,374 — black

3,041 — red
4,407 — blue
2,376 — yellow

9,065 — blue
9,764 — orange
8,255 — blue

Find the year man first walked on the moon. Add that number to the year it is now.

Styles Change

Add. Match the sums to show the hats and shoes that go together.

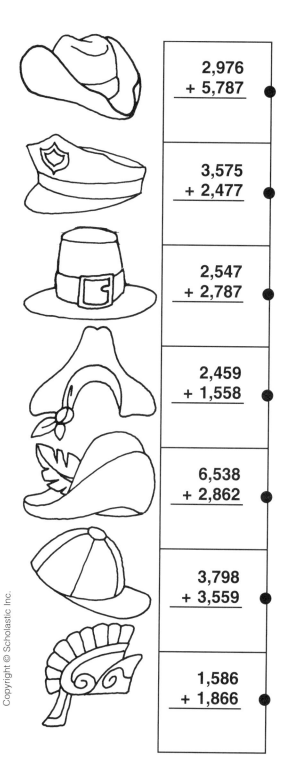

2,976 + 5,787	2,386 + 3,666
3,575 + 2,477	1,278 + 2,739
2,547 + 2,787	2,645 + 4,712
2,459 + 1,558	3,885 + 4,878
6,538 + 2,862	1,665 + 1,787
3,798 + 3,559	3,655 + 1,679
1,586 + 1,866	2,766 + 6,634

Dynamite Dominoes

Color the connecting squares that equal the same amount the same color.
Remember, 1 thousand equals 10 hundreds.

• • • • • thousands	**20** hundreds	**10** hundreds	• thousand	• • • • thousands
50 hundreds	• • • • • • • • • thousands	**90** hundreds	• • • • • thousands	**40** hundreds
30 hundreds	**70** hundreds	• • • • • • • • • thousands	**10** hundreds	**20** hundreds
• • • • thousands	• • • • thousands	• • • • • • thousands	**60** hundreds	• • thousands

Add. Write the number.

thousands		hundreds		tens		ones		
3	+	1	+	6	+	7	=	
5	+	7	+	0	+	3	=	
6	+	0	+	3	+	9	=	
4	+	5	+	8	+	4	=	
9	+	9	+	4	+	0	=	

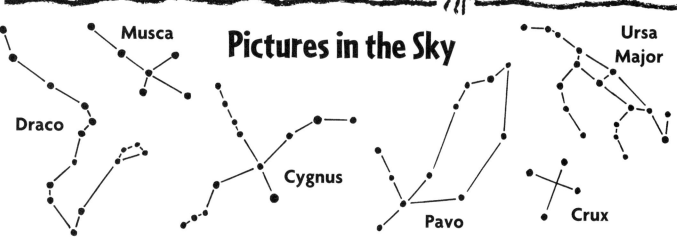

Pictures in the Sky

Subtract. Draw a line between matching sums to connect the Latin and English names for each constellation.

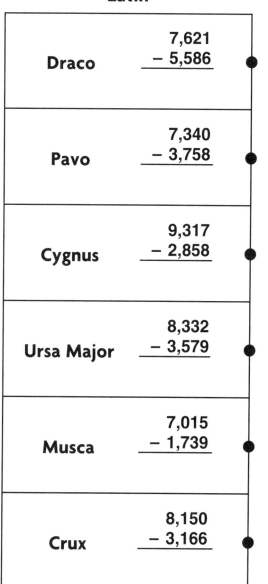

Latin

Draco	7,621 − 5,586
Pavo	7,340 − 3,758
Cygnus	9,317 − 2,858
Ursa Major	8,332 − 3,579
Musca	7,015 − 1,739
Crux	8,150 − 3,166

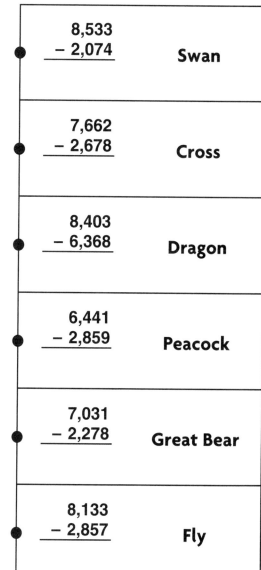

English

8,533 − 2,074	**Swan**
7,662 − 2,678	**Cross**
8,403 − 6,368	**Dragon**
6,441 − 2,859	**Peacock**
7,031 − 2,278	**Great Bear**
8,133 − 2,857	**Fly**

Imaginary Lines

Subtract.

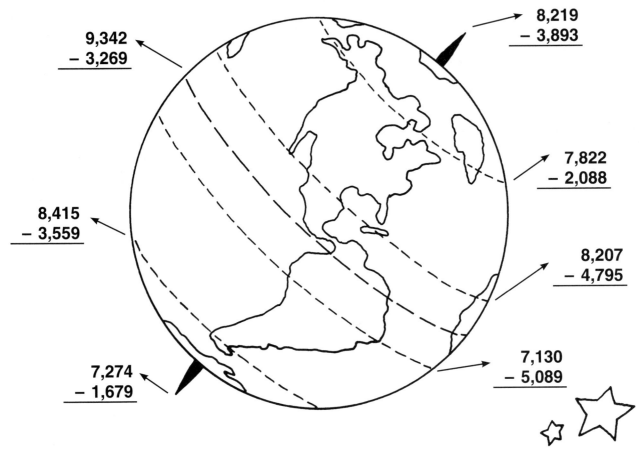

9,342
− 3,269

8,219
− 3,893

7,822
− 2,088

8,415
− 3,559

8,207
− 4,795

7,274
− 1,679

7,130
− 5,089

Find the sum of the digits in each answer to identify each global marking. Label them.

7	Tropic of Capricorn
10	Tropic of Cancer
15	North Pole
16	Equator
19	Arctic Circle
23	Antarctic Circle
24	South Pole

Name _____

Did You Know?

Add or subtract. Write the letter for the matching number below to find out whose face is on the $50 bill.

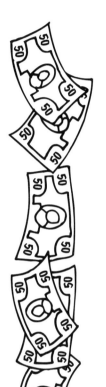

S. $27.99 + $63.84	**L.** $25.59 + $44.96	**R.** $71.90 − $59.17
E. $13.88 + $28.08	**S.** $80.31 − $46.16	**S.** $25.79 + $38.51
T. $53.97 − $29.09	**Y.** $27.66 + $43.74	**N.** $32.48 + $17.77
S. $94.33 − $56.34	**U.** $13.88 + $18.88	**G.** $68.74 − $55.29

A. $63.89 + $26.53

$32.76 $70.55 $71.40 $64.30 $91.83 $41.96 $37.99

$34.15 $13.45 $12.73 $90.42 $50.25 $24.88

Name _____

Long, Long Ago

Add or subtract. Use the chart to color the picture.

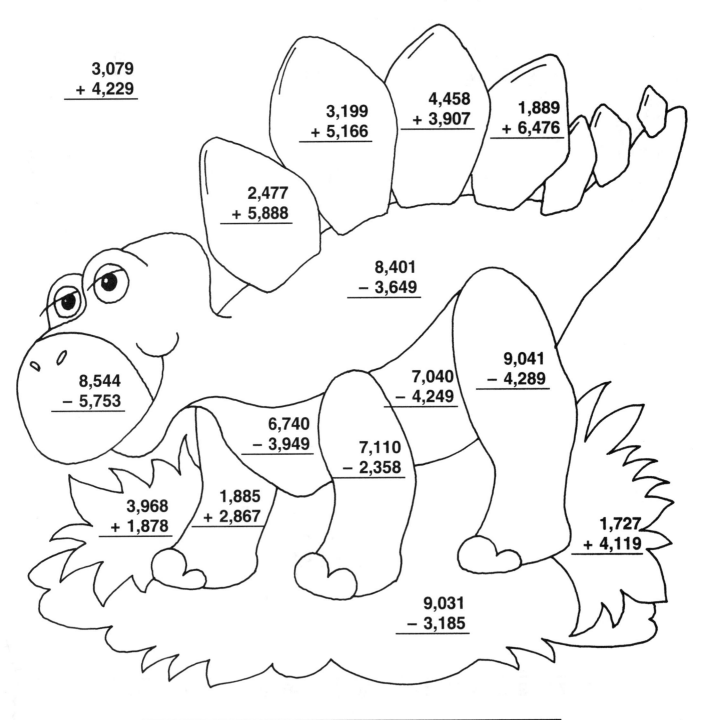

3,079
+ 4,229

2,477
+ 5,888

3,199
+ 5,166

4,458
+ 3,907

1,889
+ 6,476

8,401
− 3,649

8,544
− 5,753

6,740
− 3,949

7,110
− 2,358

7,040
− 4,249

9,041
− 4,289

3,968
+ 1,878

1,885
+ 2,867

9,031
− 3,185

1,727
+ 4,119

green	brown	yellow	pink	blue
5846	4752	8365	2791	7308

Name _____

Classy Animals

In the 1700s, a Swedish botanist devised a system for classifying plants and animals. The system's basic design is still being used today. To learn the botanist's name, add or subtract each problem.

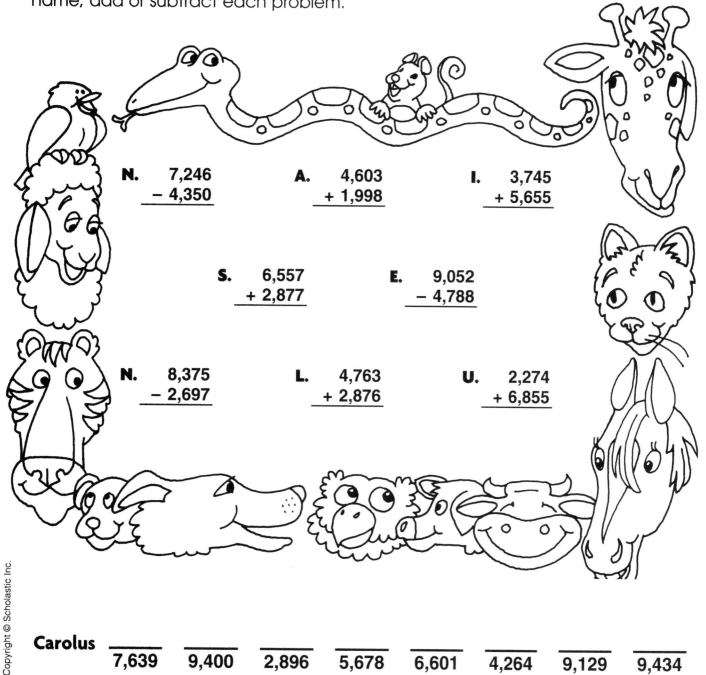

N. 7,246
− 4,350

A. 4,603
+ 1,998

I. 3,745
+ 5,655

S. 6,557
+ 2,877

E. 9,052
− 4,788

N. 8,375
− 2,697

L. 4,763
+ 2,876

U. 2,274
+ 6,855

Carolus _____ _____ _____ _____ _____ _____ _____ _____
7,639   9,400   2,896   5,678   6,601   4,264   9,129   9,434

 There are over 1.5 million kinds of animals. There are about 4,000 kinds of amphibians, 4,500 kinds of mammals, 6,500 kinds of reptiles, 9,700 kinds of birds, 21,000 kinds of fish, and 1 million kinds of insects! How many more kinds of fish have been identified than birds?

Name _____

Fun With Numbers

Add or subtract. Then write the problem's letter above its matching answer below.

W.
2,376
+ 2,784

O.
8,500
− 2,763

T.
4,401
− 2,550

A.
2,763
+ 3,857

E.
6,345
− 2,660

H.
8,455
− 1,867

!
4,672
+ 3,885

M.
8,304
− 2,541

M.
2,463
+ 4,908

A.
1,074
+ 5,988

E.
4,365
− 1,478

S.
3,453
+ 2,778

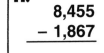
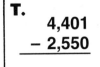

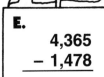

___ ___ ___ ___ **is**
5,763 7,062 1,851 6,588

___ ___ ___ ___ ___ ___ ___ ___
6,620 5,160 2,887 6,231 5,737 7,371 3,685 8,557

Page 4
18, 7, 15; 18, 16, 14; 18, 15, 17; 8, 18, 15; 18, 9, 15; 12, 9, 18; 16, 11, 17; 13, 11, 18; 14, 18, 16; 4, 9, 2; 3 + 10 = 13 ships

Page 5
14, 8, 2, 5, 11, spade; 2, 7, 11, axe; 4, 2, 5, 1, 17, radio; 14, 2, 10, 11, 4, saber; Put an X on the radio and saber.

Page 6
7, 4, 13, 10, 15, 5, 9, 16, 8, 12, 3, 6, 18, 11, 14; Charity, Constance, Edward, Humility, Jasper, Oceanus, Peregrine, Priscilla, Prudence, Remember, Resolve, Samuel, Solomon, Susan, Thomas

Page 7
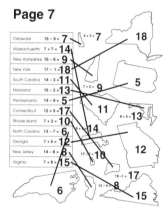

Page 8
75, 23, 98, 86, 47, 34, 75, 99, AMERICAN; 86, 98, 33, 78, 64, 87, 32, 47, 78, 99, REVOLUTION; 64, 47, 51, 98, 86, 32, 21, LIBERTY; 51, 98, 64, 64; BELL

Page 9
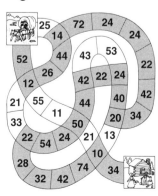

Page 10
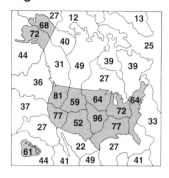

Page 11
Check that each student has circled the correct number of stars.

3 tens, 4 ones, 34; 4 tens, 5 ones, 45; 2 tens, 7 ones, 27; 7 tens, 0 ones, 70; 5 tens, 3 ones, 54; 6 tens, 5 ones 65; 3 tens, 6 ones, 36; 8 tens, 0 ones, 80; 13, 13 + 50 = 63, 6 tens, 3 ones

Page 12
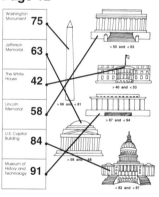

Page 13
52, 53, 82, 61, 96, 52, 82, LINCOLN; 37, 83, 42, 42, 83, 78, 66, 96, 82, JEFFERSON; 98, 72, 64, 65, 53, 82, 45, 47, 96, 82, WASHINGTON

Page 14
37: 3 tens 7 ones, 2 tens 17 ones; 52: 5 tens 2 ones, 4 tens, 12 ones; 85: 8 tens 5 ones, 7 tens 15 ones; 43: 4 tens 3 ones, 3 tens 13 ones; 68: 6 tens 8 ones, 5 tens 18 ones; 26: 2 tens 6 ones, 1 ten 16 ones

Page 15

Page 16
52 − 13 = 39, 68 − 29 = 39, 76 − 48 = 28, 68 − 39 = 29, 90 − 61 = 29; 81 − 42 = 39, 75 − 49 = 26, 72 − 37 = 35; 75 − 29 = 46, 90 − 13 = 77; 52 − 48 = 4, 81 − 39 = 42; 72 − 49 = 23, 76 − 37 = 39

Page 17
30 − 23 = 7, 80 − 58 = 22; 70 − 51 = 19, 40 − 35 = 5; 20 − 12 = 8, 90 − 64 = 26; 60 − 47 = 13, 50 − 26 = 24

Page 18
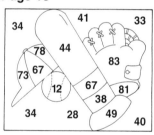

Check students' coloring.
32, 34, 36, 38, 40, 42, 44, 46, 48, 50

Page 19
16 + 87 = 103, 57 + 11 = 68, 91 + 45 = 136, 39 + 49 = 133, 68 + 29 = 97, 25 + 73 = 98, 83 + 32 = 115, 44 + 58 = 102, 72 + 66 = 138; 87 − 16 = 71, 57 − 11 = 46, 91 − 45 = 46, 94 − 39 = 55, 68 − 29 = 39, 73 − 25 = 48, 83 − 32 = 51, 58 − 44 = 14, 72 − 66 = 6;
A. 41; B. 90; C. 34; D. 58

Page 20
24, 91, 47, 53, 16, 92, 65, 38
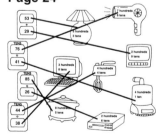

Page 21
56 + 38 = 94, 18 + 24 + 35 = 77, 38 + 34 + 18 = 90, 47 + 24 = 71; 90 − 77 = 13, 94 − 77 = 17, 90 − 71 = 19, 94 − 71 = 23; 47 − 38 = 9; 56 − 18 = 38; 252

Page 22
S. 75; I. 24; A. 65; R. 38; R. 84; W. 57; H. 58; I. 64; U. 33; O. 72; L. 51; M. 34; B. 71; L. 80; G. 69; U. 48; WILLIAM BURROUGHS

Page 23
324 + 632 = 956, 241 + 551 792; 155 + 331 = 486, 213 + 313 = 526; 415 + 322 = 737, 143 + 146 = 289, 202 + 216 = 418, 431 + 422 = 853; 142 + 233 = 375, 541 + 134 = 675, 335 + 333 = 668, 712 + 232 = 944; 220 + 314 = 534, 514 + 334 = 848, 224 + 143 = 367, 416 + 132 = 548; Joe brought $5.40, and Ellie brought $4.35.

Page 24

200, 40, 7, 247; 400, 70, 6, 476; 300, 90, 2, 392; 100, 90, 3, 193; 500, 60, 1, 561

Page 25
40, 50, 60; 80, 20, 70; 9 hundreds, 30 tens; 60 tens, 1 hundred; 80 tens, 9 hundreds

Page 26

954	427	554
684	349	364
945	844	472
457	574	942
473	424	842

970	373	872
723	577	884
507	476	397
743	771	712
575	674	974

Page 27

574	534	558
346	506	763
852	523	945
952	524	965
897	563	723

726	622	923
327	288	525
628	824	421
826	842	428
724	725	527

Page 28

534 − 275 = 259; 467 − 278 = 189; 392 − 296 = 96; 625 − 366 = 259, 988 − 589 = 399, 735 − 367 = 368; 854 − 397 = 457, 564 − 498 = 66, 339 − 249 = 90

Page 29

Check students' coloring.

Page 30

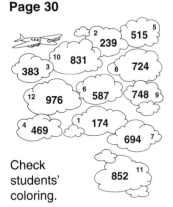

Check students' coloring.

Page 31

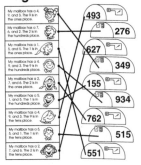

Page 32

A. 517 + 525 = 1,042; B. 614 + 478 = 1,092; C. 709 + 253 = 962; D. 1,363, **722** E. 709 − 385 = 324, 517 − 463 = 54, 525 − 385 = 140; 253 + 517 + 254 + 614 = 1,638

Page 33

A. 496 − 188 = 308; B. 956 − 668 = 288; C. 547 + 239 = 786; D. 379 + 345 = 724; E. 723 − 162 = 561; F. 422 − 215 = 207; G. 957 − 688 = 269; H. 884 + 834 = 1,718; I. 956 − 578 = 378

Page 34

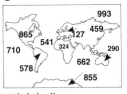

Check labeling.

Page 35

5,063; 3,721; 3,827; 8,749; ALPS; 8,789; 2,429; 3,012; 5,642; 2,351; ROCKY; 2,429; 5,234; 5,063; 8,789; 5,642; OZARK; 5,063; 6,348; 4,907; 7,483; 8,749; ANDES; 2.846

Page 36

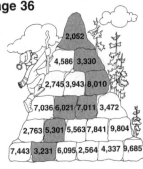

Page 37

F. $39.96; N. $79.96; N. $99.48; R. $66.99; K. $86.99; A. $79.77; L. $88.99; I. $97.00; FRANKLIN; 5, 2, 8, 1, 3, 7, 9, 4, 6

Page 38

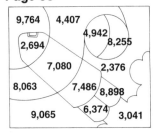

Page 39

Page 40

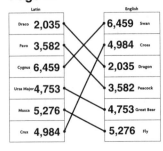

3,167; 5,703; 6,039; 4,584; 9,940

Page 41

Latin		English	
Draco	2,035	6,459	Swan
Pavo	3,582	4,984	Cross
Cygnus	6,459	2,035	Dragon
Ursa Major	4,753	3,582	Peacock
Musca	5,276	4,753	Great Bear
Crux	4,984	5,276	Fly

Page 42

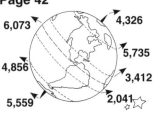

Check labeling.

Page 43

S. $91.83, L. $70.55, R. $12.73; E. $41.96, S. $34.15. S. $64.30; T. $24.88, Y. $71.40, N. $50.25; S. $37.99; U. $32.76; G. $13.45; A. $90.42; ULYSSES S. GRANT

Page 44

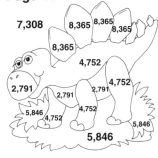

Check students' coloring.

Page 45

N. 2,896; A. 6,601; I. 9,400; S. 9,434; E. 4,264; N. 5,678; L. 7,639; E. 9,129; LINNAEUS; 11,300

Page 46

MATH is AWESOME!